Lisa Gail Rittberger
12 Holmes Dale
Albany, New York

HOUDON F 1785

Martha Washington

LeT's Go To

Illustrated by

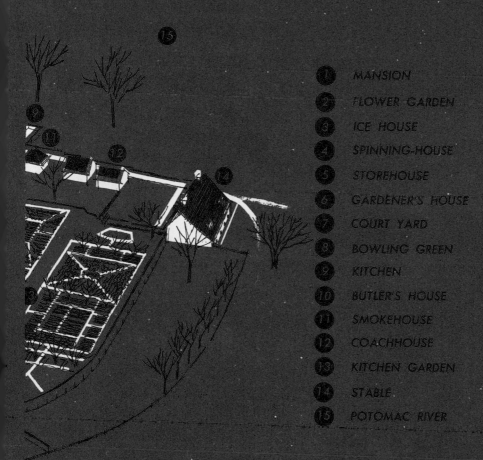

Mt. VERNON

By MARY JO BORRESON
Moneta Barnett

G. P. Putnam's Sons
New York

Published simultaneously in the Dominion of Canada by
Longmans, Green and Company, Toronto.
The author and artist wish to thank the staff of The Mount Vernon Ladies'
Association of the Union for their help in preparing this book.

Every year more than a million people come from far and near to visit Mount Vernon. Kings and laborers, queens and housewives, older people who have retired and younger folks who are still in school, all come for the same reason—to see where George Washington lived.

Mount Vernon has been full of visitors for more than two hundred years. Not only did George and Martha Washington often entertain friends but they also received many prominent men of the day who came to call on important business. There was such a constant stream of visitors that Washington, in a letter to his mother, once compared his home to "a well-resorted tavern."

All of his adult life, George Washington wanted to settle down at Mount Vernon and lead the life of a farmer. But his career in public life often took him away from home. Sometimes he was gone for years, as when he was Commanding General of the Revolutionary Army. Even when he was away, however, he made certain that Mount Vernon was being well cared for and improved because he was very proud of his home.

Lawrence Washington

"No estate in United America," Washington once wrote, "is more pleasantly situated than this. It lies in a high, dry and healthy Country 300 miles by water from the Sea . . . on one of the finest Rivers [the Potomac] in the world."

George Washington was not the original owner of Mount Vernon, but the land had been in his family for many years. Lawrence Washington, George's elder half brother who owned the estate before George, named it Mount Vernon in honor of Admiral Edward Vernon under whom he had served at sea.

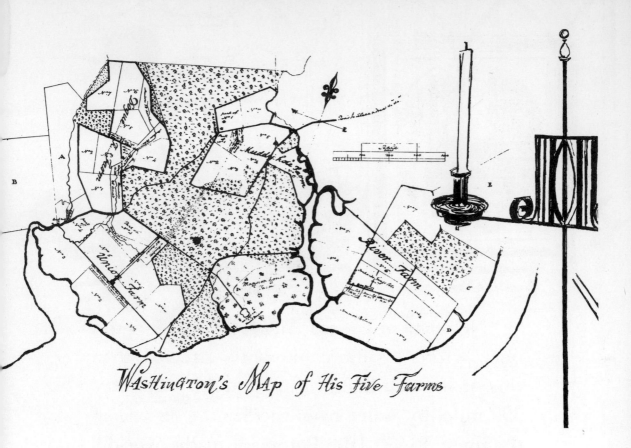

Washington's Map of His Five Farms

The estate consisted of five farms, each of which was like a tiny village, complete with its own overseer, workers, livestock, equipment and buildings. When Washington was at home, he regularly visited the five farms to inspect them, to plan improvements and to direct the work. When he had to be away from Mount Vernon, he received weekly reports from his

manager on the progress of his farms; and he wrote long letters in reply.

George Washington and his family lived on what was called the Mansion House Farm. The other four farms were devoted mainly to the growing of crops and timber; but at the mansion farm only small areas of ground were planted, with the idea of experimenting with new crops and new methods of farming.

When Washington became owner of Mount Vernon in 1754, the Mansion House was one and one half stories high, with a chimney at each end. By 1787, it was two and one half stories high; and at each end were additions to allow for a banquet hall on one side and private rooms for General and Mrs. Washington on the other side. The outer walls of the house were made of wooden planks cut to look like blocks of stone; and when the walls were freshly painted, sand was applied to the surface. A cupola was added to the roof; and last of all, a weather vane was placed on top of the cupola.

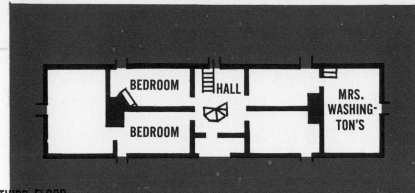

THIRD FLOOR

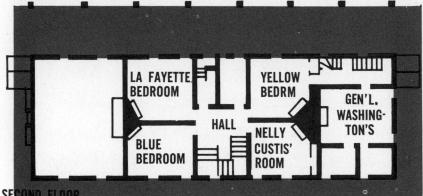

SECOND FLOOR

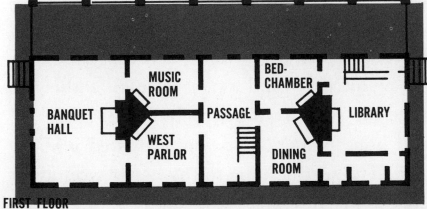

FIRST FLOOR

Floor Plans of Mount Vernon

You might think that the Mansion House could have been remodeled more quickly; but George Washington wanted only the very best for his home, and he went to considerable trouble to get it. Many of his supplies had to come from England; and occasionally shipments were lost at sea or damaged when they did arrive, so that progress was slow.

What you see and enjoy today is Mount Vernon as it appeared at the end of Washington's lifetime, after many years of continuous planning, designing, repairing and remodeling.

Those who came to visit the Washingtons caught their first glimpse of Mount Vernon as they passed through the "west gate" three-quarters of a mile from the home. Looking across a soft green meadow and up a little hill, they could see the west front of the beautiful white mansion house with its red roof crowned with a cupola. The road leading to the house wound

off through shady woods before it again brought
the visitor within view of the Washingtons'
home. At this spot was a smooth bowling green,
enclosed by "serpentines," or winding drive-
ways, which led to the courtyard.

Today you pass through north entrance gates which are much closer to the bowling green, but to the west you can still look downhill and see the two little gatehouses where guests of old made their entrance.

George Washington would undoubtedly be pleased to see Mount Vernon today, for it is as he planned it and worked to make it look. The serpentine avenues are lined with the same kinds of trees listed in his original plan, and several are those which he himself started from seedlings. The flower gardens and kitchen gardens on either side of the serpentines are planted with the same kinds of flowers and fruits, vegetables and herbs which were grown there years ago. Honeysuckle climbs and spreads as it did when Washington planted it at each column of the covered walks which lead from the main house to the outbuildings on either side.

In the middle of the circular courtyard lawn you can find the original sundial. And topping the cupola on the roof is the weather vane, in the form of a dove of peace, which Washington added as the final decoration to the outside of his house.

All these things were seen by the eighteenth-century visitor as he rode up the serpentine toward the courtyard. There he was met; and while his horse was taken down the south lane to the stable, he was led through the west front door into the "passage." This is a central hall which stretches from the west or courtyard front through to the east front which overlooks the Potomac River. (Mount Vernon has no back — just two sides and two fronts!) The passage or hall was often used as a living room in warm weather because there was a refreshing breeze stirring when both west and east doors were opened.

Today, because of the problem of moving many people through the mansion so that they won't bump each other, you are asked to enter the house through a door leading directly from the courtyard into the banquet hall, Washington's addition on the north end of his home.

Although the furniture has been moved away from the center of the banquet hall so that you can walk easily through the room, you can still imagine what it looked like years ago with dinner guests seated at a handsome table set with white linen, gleaming silver and sparkling crystal. If the day were chill, a coal fire would be burning in the fireplace, its flames reflected in the large mirrors hanging on the wall.

The banquet hall was a room in which Washington took great pride. The marble mantel over the fireplace and the three porcelain vases displayed on top were the gifts of an English friend. Carved on the mantelpiece are scenes of country life, quite suitable for a gentleman farmer; and on the ceiling are plaster decorations in which models of farming tools make up part of the design.

Directly opposite the fireplace you admire a large and beautiful window, hung with white dimity curtains and green satin overdrapes, just a few shades deeper than the green of the wall-paper.

On either side of the banquet hall fireplace is a door. One leads you to the west parlor where the family played cards and Martha Washington sometimes served tea to her visitors. Over the fireplace mantel is a landscape painting, above which is carved and painted the Washington family's coat of arms. On the walls are portraits which hung here during Washington's lifetime.

The other door leads you from the banquet hall to the little parlor or music room. Washington wrote, "I can neither sing one of the songs, nor raise a single note on any instrument." Nevertheless, he enjoyed both listening to music and dancing to it.

In the music room at Mount Vernon you come upon a harpsichord which George Washington ordered from London for his wife's granddaughter, Nelly Custis. It's very likely that he and Mrs. Washington often sat in the evening listening to Nelly play — even as parents do today. A book of Nelly's music is open on the rack of the harpsichord for you to see.

The Washingtons were very fond of children. At the time of their marriage, Martha Custis Washington already had two children whose father had died some time before. Patsy and Jackie Custis found George Washington to be a very devoted stepfather, and they loved living at Mount Vernon. Only Jackie lived to adulthood. After his death at the end of the American Revolution, the Washingtons took Jackie's two younger children to live with them. From that time on, George Washington Parke Custis and Eleanor Parke Custis (called "Nelly") were known as "the children of Mount Vernon."

Both the music room and the west parlor have doors opening onto the passage, where several things are of special interest to children today just as they were to the children of Mount Vernon. One is a model of the Bastille, carved from a stone from that ancient fort in Paris where prisoners were often held without trial before the French Revolution. Another is the big key to the main door of the Bastille.

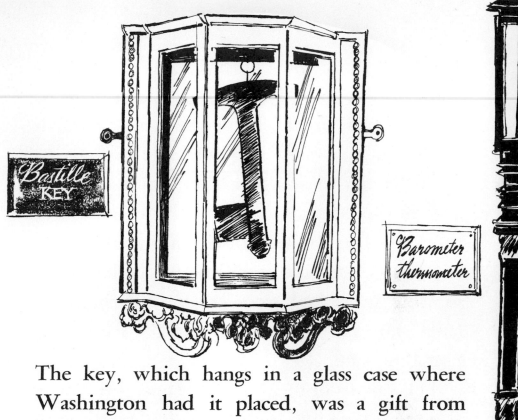

The key, which hangs in a glass case where Washington had it placed, was a gift from General Lafayette. Also hanging in the passage is a combination barometer-thermometer by which Washington could read the weather conditions.

When the day was fine, the Washingtons could open the east door to enjoy the pleasant weather from the porch. Standing on this long front porch, you see a lovely green lawn and and park which slope down to the river.

Cattle, sheep and horses were allowed to graze on the grounds of the estate. But to keep them away from the house, Washington built brick "ha-ha" walls. On one side of a ha-ha wall, the earth is level with the top of the wall; and on the other, it is level with the bottom of the wall. The animals could neither jump nor step high enough to reach the upper level and so were prevented from grazing on the front lawn. You can see these brick walls when you visit the estate.

The east front of Mount Vernon is the view you most often find in pictures. The porch with its eight square columns, English flagstone flooring and long row of Windsor chairs, was used for entertaining much as our patios are used today. It was also here in the protection of the porch roof that the Washingtons took their exercise when bad weather made walking or riding undesirable.

Rain or shine, however, there were always visitors to the "well-resorted tavern." Some, it's true, came just out of curiosity to see where the famous Washington lived. But you must remember that Mount Vernon was located on the roadway between the northern and southern colonies. Since in those days there were no roadside motels in which to spend the night while making a journey, it was common for travelers to turn in at the nearest gate when nightfall came, to ask lodging even from people whom they'd never met.

Welcoming a guest, known or unknown, meant somewhat more in the eighteenth century than it does today. It meant providing him (and his servants) with not only food and lodging but also possible repairs to his carriage, to his horses' harnesses or even to his boots or shoes. Sometimes it meant the laundering of his soiled clothes!

Because horses and carriages didn't move according to a regular schedule and because even the landing of boats and ships on the river depended on the winds and tides, guests might arrive at any hour of the day or night. There was a downstairs bedroom off the passage which was kept ready for those who might arrive late at night so that people asleep on the second floor need not be disturbed.

Also off the passage you find the family dining room. This room would have been too small for a large gathering of dinner guests but was big enough for the regular members of the household. In the dining room, along with more formal furniture, you can see a little high chair said to have been used by the children of Mount Vernon when they were very small.

The addition which Washington had built on the south end of the house made space on the first floor for two rooms. The first was a small pantry near the family dining room. From a connecting hall, a door opens onto a covered

walk leading to the kitchen. You notice that the kitchen is a separate building, as were most eighteenth-century kitchens. In the pantry was kept the tableware which was in regular use. Today the pantry is furnished as it was then, the most "romantic" item being a small table on which it is believed that George and Martha Washington ate their wedding breakfast.

The other room provided by the new south addition was the library. This was Washington's study and office. Here he wrote in his diary, received reports from the overseers of the five farms, kept his account books, penned his personal and business letters, and wrote speeches and documents which became important in forming a new government in America. Today, you can see the shelves lined with many of the books from Washington's own library. There are books on farming, military matters, religion, poetry, fiction, history, and geography. You can see Washington's large globe of the world and several surveying instruments which will remind you of the days when as a young man he went into the wilderness to survey and chart the land.

Directly over the library is the Washingtons' bedroom with two adjoining dressing rooms. A side stairway between the first and second floors permitted General and Mrs. Washington to have a little privacy in a house always full of people. In this room, which overlooks the woods and winding river toward the south, George Washington died on December 14, 1799.

The bedroom is furnished with the Washingtons' four-poster bed, Mrs. Washington's desk, the General's shaving and dressing table and other items which were in the room when it was occupied. At the foot of the bed you see a trunk with General Washington's name on it. This is the trunk in which he kept his personal things during the Revolutionary War.

Today you reach the bedroom by walking
through the Yellow Room and a tiny hallway
which was once one of Mrs. Washington's clos-
ets. To make passage possible, the back wall of
the closet has been removed. This is one of the
very few changes that have been made in the
house plan of Mount Vernon since Washington's day.

There are five other bedrooms on the second floor. At the head of the main stairway is the Blue Bedroom in which you can see the trunk Martha Washington used when she traveled to and from the winter quarters of the Army during the American Revolution. Another bedroom is called the Lafayette Room because it was used by General Lafayette whenever he visited Mount Vernon. Across the hall are the Yellow Room and Nelly Custis' room where you can see the little crib used by Nelly's first baby, who was born at Mount Vernon in 1799. There is another smaller bedroom next to the attic stairway.

On the stair landing leading to the attic, you can see several leather fire buckets lettered with George Washington's name. Washington brought these with him from his home in Philadelphia where he lived while he was our first President. Before modern fire-fighting equipment, each city home was required to have a supply of fire buckets, the number depending upon the size of the house. Leather was used for the buckets because it could stand rough treatment better than wood.

Because it is not furnished, the attic at Mount Vernon is closed to visitors. In Washington's time, some of the attic rooms were used as bedrooms, others for storage. From the attic, a circular staircase leads to the cupola from which the Washingtons could enjoy the view of the river, the distant Maryland shore, and the rolling Virginia countryside which surrounded the estate.

Near the house, on the north side, is a building now used as an office. In Washington's time some of the servants lived here. Along the north lane you can see the gardener's house, used at different times as an infirmary, a shoemaker's shop and a tailor's shop. Next you come to the storehouse (now containing a vault in which are kept many of Washington's important official papers). There are also an icehouse (where part of Mount Vernon's modern fire-fighting equipment is now kept) and the spinning house in which servants worked the wool, flax and cotton fibers grown on the farm. "Necessary houses," or outside bathrooms, were located near the gardens.

Past the flower garden, which lies beyond the north serpentine driveway, you see the greenhouse whose wings served as living quarters for some of the servants. At the far end of the flower garden stands a small white eight-sided building known as the schoolhouse. To balance the ground plan, Washington placed a toolhouse at the far end of the kitchen garden, which lies on the other side of the south serpentine.

All of the planting areas at Mount Vernon were laid out and tended with great care. The gardens today are planted with flowers and vegetables known to have been grown in eighteenth-century Virginia gardens; and they are outlined with boxwood hedges, of which Washington was especially fond. Fruit trees are trained to grow against the brick walls and along the walks, just as they grew many years ago.

Washington once wrote: "Tell the gardener I shall expect everything that a garden ought to produce, in the most ample manner." And so every kind of vegetable and herb that was needed by the cooks was cultivated.

At the head of the south lane you will see the kitchen and its wellhouse. Eighteenth-century kitchens were separated from the main house to lessen the danger of fire and to keep cooking odors from filling the living quarters. Because there was often the need to serve a large company, Mrs. Washington's staff included two cooks, two waiters, and a butler who were supervised by a housekeeper. Breakfast was served at seven, dinner at three, tea at six; and supper usually followed at nine. As a result, the kitchen was always a busy place and its great open-hearth fireplace and wall oven were in almost constant use.

Today you can see the same large iron mortar — which Mrs. Washington's cooks used for grinding corn and the crane with which they could put the cooking containers into position over the fire without burning their fingers. In a rack over the fireplace stand several pewter plates with hot-water compartments similar to baby dishes of today. Nearby are butter churns,

candle molds, and other utensils of the kind used in the eighteenth century.

Across the south lane you find the butler's house and storeroom, and down the lane are the smokehouse and the washhouse with its drying green behind. (Clotheslines and well ropes were made of horsehair, because it was strong and did not stretch.)

Farther down the south lane in the coach house, you can see a handsome coach once owned by Washington's friend, Samuel Powel.

At the foot of the south lane is the brick stable in which horses were sheltered and cared for. They grazed in open pasture and in the grassy paddock beyond the stable. In the coach compartment of the stable you see a two-wheeled riding chair like the one George Washington owned. The stable is outfitted with the kinds of harnesses, saddles, currying equipment and tools in use during Washington's time.

As you continue down the hill, you follow a path which leads to the tomb where the Washingtons are buried. The original tomb was closer to the river, but even in Washington's own time it was in need of repair; and the General's will directed that a new one be built on the site where millions of people now come to pay their respects to the "Father of his Country."

The warm hospitality which George and Martha Washington offered to everyone was continued by their family after the Washingtons died. But it became too expensive to take care of the increasing number of visitors. As a result, Mount Vernon was sold to The Mount Vernon Ladies' Association of the Union, an organization founded in 1853 for the purpose of purchasing the home of George Washington and keeping it as a national shrine.

When you visit Mount Vernon, you may come by car or bus; or you may take one of the boats which journey down the Potomac River from Washington, D. C., and tie up at the modern wharf which has been built on the site of George Washington's own boat landing. No matter how you travel, you will see Mount Vernon standing as proud and inviting as it did when George and Martha Washington made it their home.

GLOSSARY

AMPLE — plentiful.

BAROMETER — an instrument for predicting changes of weather.

BOWLING GREEN — a flat lawn for playing bowls, a game very much like modern bowling.

COAT OF ARMS — a group of pictures which identify a family.

CUPOLA — an enclosed lookout placed on top of a building.

CURRYING EQUIPMENT — tools used to comb and dress the hair or coat of a horse.

DIMITY — a fine cord cotton fabric.

DOCUMENT — an original or official paper.

FLAGSTONE — any hard stone that splits into pieces suitable for paving.

INFIRMARY — a place where sick people stay to be nursed.

OVERSEER — a supervisor or someone "in charge" of others.

PLANKS — heavy thick boards.

RESORTED — visited.

SHRINE — a place which is much respected.

WINDSOR CHAIR — a type of wooden chair popular especially in eighteenth-century England and in the American Colonies.

Some personal items of the Washingtons